MARRIAGE KILLERS: 7 Surefire Strategies to Ruin YOUR RELATIONSHIP... IF THAT'S *WHAT YOU WANT*

Dr. John Page

iUniverse, Inc.
Bloomington

Marriage Killers: 7 Surefire Strategies to Ruin Your Relationship...
If That's What You Want

iUniverse books may be ordered through booksellers or by contacting:

iUniverse
1663 Liberty Drive
Bloomington, IN 47403
www.iuniverse.com
1-800-Authors (1-800-288-4677)

ISBN: 978-1-4759-1436-8 (sc)
ISBN: 978-1-4759-1437-5 (ebk)

Printed in the United States of America

iUniverse rev. date: 04/27/2012

Dedicated to Jay and Sandra:
Your marriage is a tangible proof that
love, sacrifice, and respect
do in fact make a strong marriage.
You are my heros.

Contents

Introduction

One out of two marriages ultimately fail, shout the statistical polls. Magazine covers tout the latest marriage guru with their perfect points to make your marriage stronger, healthier, or sexier. The marriage and relationship section at your favorite bookseller is chock-full of how-to titles for saving your marriage, divorce-proofing your relationship, and meeting spousal needs, even if they are from a different planet.

Most self-help books on marriage give you points or strategies to work on. For instance, if you work on this communication point, your marriage will be better. They typically focus on issues of money, sex, communication, friends, relatives, and interests, to name the most popular ones. The idea seems to be that if both people in the marriage will do the plan, or work the strategies, or follow the sample talking points, then their marriage will strengthen and remain intact. This philosophy is based on a weak assumption that both people in the marriage actually want the marriage to work; they are intending to stay true to the marriage; or that they are willing to work out any problem or issue because they want to enjoy a lifetime love.

Statistics seem to show that that is not the case. So why keep wasting our time? People give up on their marriages and split for some of the most inane reasons:

- "Irreconcilable differences," which is quasi-speak for "We just didn't love each other enough to really try and work it out, or compromise, or cease our own self-centered stubbornness."
- "We grew apart," which is code for "We kept seeking our own self-interest, selfishly refused to grow together, and pointedly decided to do what we wanted to do, over and over."
- "We wanted different things," which is silly talk to cover the reality that the two people had no intention of staying together for any length of time anyway, but just got married for the fun, thrill, or convenience of it.

How do I know this? Because I've invested countless hours with couples before they are married. Because I've spent even more hours listening to couples after they are married, telling me why they don't think it's going to work out. With more than 15 years of training and experience, I've seen what destroys marriages.

Since the statistics on marriage and relational failures make it pretty clear that many people considering marriage don't have any intention of seeing it through, I've created a list of *Marriage Killers: Seven Sure-fire Strategies for Ruining Your Relationship.* If you haven't already picked up on it, I make tremendous use of sarcasm to illustrate these Strategies, in order to shine the light on how absurd this behavior really is. If you are turned off by such sarcasm, that is unfortunate, but I employ it as a tool to break through silly excuses and lame assumptions regarding marriage.

Follow these simple methods and you can easily demolish your vows, diminish spousal love, and deter any growth in what was once a lifetime relationship—if that's what you really want to do. If your goal is killing your marriage, then adhere to these strategies.

WARNING: However, if you intend to take your wedding vows seriously and work hard at making your marriage last, then this book is not for you. Don't buy this book if you seek to see the best in your spouse, compromise as needed, or love them even when they may act unlovable. Are you planning on seeing the commitment through despite, and in spite of tough circumstances? Will you take the long-term view on marriage and realize the beauty of a life lived, through ups and downs, with your spouse? Do the words, "Until we are parted by death" have great meaning to you? If you answered yes to any of those questions, then put this book down as it is not what you want or need. You actually take marriage seriously and understand its importance, unlike the examples in this book.

This book is for people who enter marriage with an attitude of "We'll see how it goes." *Marriage Killers* is for people who look to entertainment stars as their examples of how to move in and out of multiple marriages and pairings. You'll want to read this book if you think marriage is about enjoying the other person until someone better comes along. If you enter marriage with the thought that it's your mission to change the other person into who you want them to be, this book can prove helpful. You need this book if you believe marriage is about fulfilling your needs, or that your spouse should be focused on only what you want. These Surefire Strategies are for those people who intend to use them fully. Don't hold back if you're going to use these Strategies. They only kill your marriage if you go "all-in."

The stories contained in the following chapters are true and the people described are real, but names and identities have been altered. But don't let their anonymity stop you. Just do what they did and your marriage will end before you know it. Learn from these people, as they are your personal mentors as you become a Marriage Killer.

These Surefire Strategies are numbered one through seven, but you can read them in any order. You can also use them in any order, or simultaneously if you are adept. I don't present them in order of importance. They are not linked together other than to say that if you enact all Seven Surefire Strategies, you guarantee the death of your marriage. Sometimes, as you will see in the examples, it only takes one of these Strategies to do the trick. But hey, get your money's worth and go full tilt with them.

The first Surefire Strategy is entitled "I Can't Hear You!" It represents the aspect of communication in a marriage. Here you'll learn the fine art of not communicating. In fact, don't worry about communicating, just assume your spouse knows and understands what you're thinking and feeling. Under no circumstances should you share anything vulnerable or sensitive—they'll just use it to shame you or hurt you later.

Next is "It's All Mine!" which covers the topic of finances and money in marriage. This Surefire Strategy is all about keeping what is yours, yours. Keep your money separate and hidden because your spouse will rob you blind or keep you down if you share. Feel free to run up debt for what you want—they may get stuck half the debt when you divorce.

Surefire Strategy #3 is about "Protecting Your Self." Don't let your spouse suck your life dry with all they want to do. Stop wasting time wondering about their needs or what matters to them. Relax and let their love tank run on empty. They enjoy snuggling on the couch watching a movie? No worries, you've got to go for a jog. They appreciate a verbal pat-on-the-back for accomplishing a task? Immaterial—you need to do lunch with your friends. If you do activities they enjoy, your own life force will shrivel up.

Two people in a marriage have divided tasks that they should handle. Surefire Strategy #4 reminds you of the adage, "That's Your Job!" Live in your strengths. Do only those household tasks that you enjoy doing, if any at all. Forget about "helping out," or "doing your part," or even "pitching in where needed because we're in this together." You're not a sports team, for crying out loud!

In our fifth Surefire Strategy, you are reminded to skip the articles in your favorite magazine and just stare at the photographs of naked people. After all, "They're Just Pictures!" Definitely get into porn. Skip subscribing to a magazine. Get it instantly online. Make sure you view it daily. Use it instead of a real, intimate, sexual experience with your spouse because that's always the same thing, same position (and not very often!). Better yet, just take the natural next step and have an affair. It's just sex, after all.

Your spouse has a family and you need to stay away from them and talk bad about them. If you doubt this, Surefire Strategy #6 describes the truth about "I Married You, Not Them!" Ignore your spouse's family—they're not who you married. Don't call, text, or email on special occasions like birthdays or anniversaries. For your own sake, make every effort to avoid family gatherings at holiday times, especially reunions. Remember to neglect any issues regarding their siblings or aging parents.

You need to limit your exposure to your spouse's friends. Marriage is just about the two of you; you don't need other people. Surefire Strategy #7, "Are They Coming Over Again?!" gives you tips on how to downgrade your spouse's friends. Since when do you have to be chummy with their friends? Make excuses for why you can't make it to Zach and Jennifer's party. When they want to have their group of friends over, be nasty about it, or schedule something else on top of it.

Remember to read the "Final Word," as it will reinforce the truth that if you use this book properly, it will work. You will destroy your marriage. You will successfully kill your relationship. That's what you want, right?

Surefire Strategy #1

I Can't Hear You!

Don't worry about communicating, just assume they know and understand what you're thinking and feeling.

On those few occasions when you do actually talk, make sure your comments are laced with sarcasm or cutting critiques of your spouse.

Under no circumstances should you share anything vulnerable or sensitive—they'll just use it to shame you or hurt you later.

"How'd it go today? Did you do any work today?" she remarked, as he entered the kitchen from the garage. He paused for a second, as he often did, and shook his head in shame for a half-beat, unseen by her.

"Yeah, like always," he said in a monotone, continuing on to the bedroom to change his clothes.

"Well, that's good, sweetie," she said, the sarcasm unmistakable in her tone. "We got the water, electric, and car bill today so I hope you made enough to pay for them."

He heard her, but he didn't. It was always the same thing, just about every day. He worked hard, but in the construction industry, his money came upon completion, not in steady, weekly checks like most people. Didn't she understand that? He knew she knew. He had told her as much last year when things started getting tight. He shouldn't have to tell her again, he thought, as he put on a clean pair of jeans. He remembered how she had mocked him for weeks after that, "Oh is this the one week you actually get paid?" He decided then never to share anything beyond surface information with her. It just hurt too much.

Great, she thought. He's disappeared into the bedroom and when he comes out, there'll be no talking, just like always. Doesn't he know I work hard to make this house clean and shop for food and cook dinner—on top of my work! She knew they were basically living on her meager salary and trying to make ends meet, which scared her. She was so frustrated at him, she thought, as she turned the chicken over to brown on the other side. He's gone all day, supposedly working and there's no money to show for it. I'd be happy living in a little apartment, but there's no way I'm telling him that, she said to herself. He'd go into a sulk for sure and then blame me. No, she thought, I'll just keep that bit of information inside, even if it hurts.

Charles and Candy were married young by today's standards—in their early 20s. He worked in the construction industry and she performed administrative tasks at various employers, and tried various home-based businesses. Candy would frequently build up frustration with Charles, who frequently worked late. She would say little until the bubble burst, then she'd unload with venomous cut-downs on his ability to provide for the household, or tease him. Charles, on the other hand, would just never talk—about anything. Candy was in the dark about what he was thinking about, or what emotion he felt. They existed, barely, in the same household.

♀-♂

Charles and Candy are your role models. You need to be like them for this strategy to work properly. Don't worry about norms or being polite, just refuse to share much information or feelings with your spouse. Who cares if they started it, or if you did, but do concentrate on continuing the snarky soliloquies, the sanctuary-like silences, and the stubborn refusal to say, "I'm sorry."

Regardless of whether you are husband or wife, see how much of your conversation can occur with one word responses, or even better, with a roll of the eyes, a dramatic sigh, or other expression of disgust. If asked a question, respond with a solid "Whatever." With the appropriate tone of voice and body language, "Sure," "Fine," "Uh-huh," or even "Peachy," will suffice as well.

Constantly refer back to that time when you tried to explain something and your spouse responded in the way they responded and use that as the Rosetta Stone of all future communication. They'll always do the same thing, so don't even bother seeing if it could be different this time around. Limit your spouse to the narrow instance when they ticked you off. In fact, go further and harp on that theme as often as you can so your spouse won't ever forget.

Whatever real emotions you're feeling, don't share them with the person you promised to "have and to hold from this day forward," unless, of course, the emotion is anger. Then, by all means, share it in every way possible. Whether it's through passive-aggressive communication, sarcastic cut-downs, or just plain yelling, always let anger rule your responses. Otherwise keep those feelings to yourself. You're thinking, "If my spouse and I could just sit and talk about this situation, talk it through, we'd be able to work it out." Nonsense.

Don't let yourself open up or be vulnerable with your "lifelong" love—you're just providing them with ammunition to blast you with in the next big fight. Or worst, they'll tease you about your weakness, "You're just so sensitive/high maintenance/touchy."

Let the verbal slights and wounds mount up like an emotion-laden Everest. Using therapy-speak, "Honey, when you said (insert hurtful comment), it made me feel (insert emotion)," is for losers. If they really cared, they wouldn't have said the hurtful comment in the first place. Bringing it to their attention will only aid their efforts—they now know a weak spot to hit. Telling your spouse that they hurt your feelings, or that their comments made you feel bad, only opens you up for more of the same.

Perhaps you and your spouse don't fight all that much. You don't need to tell the one you promised to "love and honor" that you love them. You said it on your wedding day, so they should just know it. Constantly telling your spouse you love him or her only lessens the value and impact of the phrase, "I love you." It only has meaning when use it rarely, if at all.

They should just discern what you're thinking or feeling. After all, you've been living in the same space for how many years? Should you really have to explain, every time, what you're thinking about the situation? Is it really necessary to clarify your purposes and intent, to confirm details and plans? Why can't they simply know, or figure it out?

♀-♂

Charles and Candy had it worked out well. The routine was set in place. He'd leave the house in the morning before she was awake so that cut out at least an hour of talking time. Neither of them would call or text each other during the day so the only time they needed to communicate was when he got home, usually after dark. But notice how they worked this perfectly to limit good downloading of each other's day, or sharing of any important information.

Charles would arrive home dreading the barrage that was coming so he would steel himself as he went in the house. Candy's resentment built all day so she was ready to fire away as soon as he was within ear's reach. He was determined not to give her any satisfaction by responding to her barbs (which was a shield against admitting that he felt like a failure). She was hell-bent on letting him know she didn't think he made enough to cover the bills (which was really covering up her insecurity of financial safety). They both followed the self-created script to the letter. They could have won awards for how perfectly they played their parts of the hating, non-communicative spouse.

He would run through his feelings in his head and only offer grunt-like responses to her comments or questions. She would only speak in the dialect of Sarcasm. Usually this evolved into a dinner in silence or, if the planets aligned just so, a scene of yelling, plates half-filled with food thrown into the sink, slamming doors, and a late-night ride around town steaming, while the other person stewed on the couch watching *Sex in the City* reruns.

This is your goal. This scenario is what you're after in your marriage, so that this Sure-Fire Strategy will work as it should. If you already haven't, begin to shut down your communication with your spouse. Or, ramp up the biting sarcasm and stinging cynicism until you start getting negative responses. Then you will know you have found the zone. Once you know how much it takes to get your spouse yelling at you, or conversely, to shut down on you, stay there. You'll be well on your way to achieving success in this first Surefire Strategy. Simply follow the guidance in this chapter and you can begin to kill your marriage. That's what you want, right?

Surefire Strategy #2

It's All Mine! (or What's Mine is Mine!)

Keep your money separate and hidden because your spouse will rob you blind or keep you down if you share.

Feel free to run up debt for what you want—they may get stuck with half the debt when you divorce.

Dixie stood in front of him with her finger at the corner of her mouth, practiced little-girl pout in place. Torsten knew what was coming. She always did this when she wanted more money. "Honey, I found a nice outfit that I know you'll like," she said. Here it comes, he thought. "I just need $100 more above my allowance," she sighed, running her finger along her lips. "It had better make you look sexy," he growled as he peeled of five Andrew Jacksons and handed them to her.

Torsten controlled the money in the marriage. Dixie never knew how much money the household had, as her meager check was direct deposited into the account. Torsten would give her a certain amount of cash each week. From that allowance, she was expected to pay for her expenses. If she wanted to purchase something, she had to come and ask Torsten for more money. Most of the time, he would release the funds, but sometimes he would not. Dixie trusted Torsten to know what money needed to be where and to run the finances so that all the bills were paid and they could live their lifestyle. It grated on her a little bit that she had to ask him for money, but she figured she could do whatever she wanted with the money she *did* get so she didn't dwell too much on the matter. After all, they lived in a nice house in a good neighborhood, had good cars, ate out at local restaurants more often than not, and enjoyed pleasant vacations.

Dixie never considered the fact that Torsten purchased a new car every two years, while her car was five years old. She didn't notice that he had at least half a dozen really nice watches on his dresser, or the five sets of high-end sunglasses, or even the many pairs of Italian leather shoes in his closet. She just figured he needed to look good as the owner of his own business.

What Dixie didn't know was that Torsten's business was plummeting in revenue. Through some financial trickery, he was paying for a lot of their lifestyle out of the debt in his business. Her paycheck was actually being used to keep them afloat. Torsten knew all this but he wasn't ever going to tell Dixie. What she didn't know wouldn't hurt her, after all, as long as bills got paid. Torsten would often tell her no for her purchases so he could buy what he wanted.

He had to look good to maintain his image. And, in his mind, he was the boss of the money in the marriage so he could do what he wanted with it and she'd just have to abide by it.

♀-♂

LaTonya and Earl had been high school sweethearts and continued their romance through college, getting married shortly after graduation. Both worked in jobs they enjoyed and were good at—blissfully living an average middle class life. After several years, Earl's job required him to travel more, so he was gone for a few days at a time, though there were several times a year where he was absent from home for a whole week. LaTonya held down the fort at home with their two kids and her full-time job. She paid the bills so she knew funds were tight but they were doing okay.

It took more than a couple of years for LaTonya to notice that Earl was extending his trips by a day or two. When he left for his trips, Earl would tell her he'd be back in a certain number of days. Yet, more often than not, he'd call her mid-trip and tell her, "Hey babe, looks like I got to stay over an extra day. Got to wrap up the final details then I'll be home." LaTonya wrote it off as the demands of the job. But, as it happened more and more, she began to ask questions in her mind. Then she began to gently ask questions of Earl, "Seems like work always goes long. Don't they plan more accurately?" Or she'd mention, "We really miss you when you're gone for so long." Earl would say the proper words but essentially he was blowing her off.

Then LaTonya found out what was happening through a series of unrelated events. And did she ever wake up to a grand surprise. Earl had created a whole other set of financials for himself, running up debt on a credit card LaTonya never knew he had. What about those extra days on the business trips? Earl was visiting strip clubs and paying for it on the mystery credit card. He was even in the process of buying a house on the other side of the city for him and his mistress that he had met on one of the business trips.

While LaTonya was using her imagination and financial skill to pay for dentist bills for the kids, Earl was living the 'Vegas life' on a separate credit card, racking up enormous debt that he had no intention of paying off. If the story just stopped there it would be a story of betrayal only and would have no place in this chapter for Surefire Strategy #2.

They got a divorce, you see. And in the state in which they lived, the debt of the couple was evenly split, regardless of who created the debt. So, while Earl was living it up, he created tens of thousands of dollars of debt that were now half the responsibility of LaTonya. She had no choice in the matter. She had to pay her half over time. It almost crippled her financially in her new, single-parent life after the divorce.

Well played, Earl. You did it the right way, my man! Brilliant move getting your own separate credit card and using it for what you want—it's your money and your life. And you don't even have to pay it all off—Latonya got stuck with it! That is the way to do it, dear readers. This Surefire Strategy will work like a charm if you follow Earl's example. Keep your spending separate and especially a secret. It's none of your spouse's business what you spend money on, or how much you spend. Your spouse should just trust you and not worry about it.

Torsten, you and Earl should team up and write a book about how to do finances in a marriage, because you got it right on the mark. Definitely keep your spouse on a tight leash financially. Only give your spouse the amount of money you want them to spend, that they are allowed to spend. Keep control of the finances, the checkbooks, the online banking, and of course any investments.

If both of you work, at the very least, you must have completely separate checking and savings accounts. Don't let the vow about "for richer, for poorer" get in the way of controlling the money you make. The ideal, of course is for you to have oversight and authority over the household finances, but work this Strategy according to your context. Use your accounts for the stuff you want, the toys, the pleasurable things like eating out, and entertainment. Let your spouse's account cover the boring stuff like utility bills and mortgage.

Try not to brag about how much money you make because your spouse may see that you make more and start asking for money. Keep that information to yourself. Money in a marriage should be separate, not shared, otherwise, you won't have the money you need for what you want.

If you start mixing your money with your spouse's into one account, your spouse will spend you dry. Ignore those who tell you that having joint accounts is one of the foundations of trust in marriage; that it strengthens the relationship because you have to make financial decisions together. That kind of advice is a crock. You're a grown adult who works hard for the money you earn. You don't need to get sign-off approval for purchases. You didn't have to prior to being married so why should you start now?

Ignore any suggestions from others that say that putting all the money in the household together is a good decision. It implies there is trust between you and your spouse—this is nonsense. Trust in money matters is not what makes a marriage work. You can't trust anyone with money, or about money, especially not the person you married. You had your own accounts prior to marriage, so why should joining in committed matrimony necessitate you getting a joint checking account? Surely not. You're living in the same place, sleeping in the same bed, but by no means should you deepen the commitment by sharing the same money.

Be like Torsten and control all financial matters, if at all possible. If you can't arrange for that scenario, then emulate Earl. Just maintain completely separate, and secret, finances. This way, you can do what you want. Stand in front of the mirror and rehearse, "What's mine is mine. It's all mine!" Remember, this Surefire Strategy is all about keeping what is yours, especially when it comes to money. Work this one properly and you'll soon be on your way to ruining your relationship, just like Torsten and Earl.

Surefire Strategy #3

Protect Your Self

*Stop wasting time wondering about their needs or what matters
to them. Relax and let their love tank run on empty. They enjoy
snuggling on the couch watching a movie? No worries, you've got to go
for a jog. They appreciate a verbal pat-on-the-back for accomplishing
a task? Immaterial—you need to do lunch with your friends. If you
only do activities they enjoy, your own life force will shrivel up.*

Terry loved his truck. Tonya wanted to surprise her husband by cleaning his truck while he was at the store with their other car. She sprayed it down to rinse off the pollen and dust, then set about the task of soaping up each section and rinsing each section before moving on. Tonya didn't want the soap to dry on the paint and leave blemishes. She knew how to wash a truck. The wheels and fenders got extra attention. Window cleaner was applied and wiped clean and clear. The truck sparkled when Tonya was done. She smiled to herself as she put the rags and bucket away. "He'll be so happy his precious truck is clean and he didn't have to do anything," she thought.

When Terry returned he noticed the truck. He knew she had cleaned it. His blood pressure rose because he just knew she hadn't done it right. "She probably just used regular soap instead of the car washing soap," he growled to himself. As he entered the house, he found her reading a magazine on the couch. "What did you clean my truck with?" he asked with some measure of force in his voice. Tonya's face just caved and tears immediately welled up in her eyes. She enjoyed doing nice things for others, especially her husband. She expected a thank you at least, not an attack. Tonya could barely get the words out, "I washed your truck so you wouldn't have to. I thought you'd appreciate it," before she ran from the room. Terry stood there fuming, completely missing out on the fact that he had just hammered his wife's love with his unappreciative verbal onslaught.

A few days earlier, Terry had come home from work and said as he walked through the kitchen, "Made a sale on one of our top accounts today. Best week I've had in a couple months." Tonya nodded and said, "That's good honey, can you empty out the dishwasher?" Terry grimaced, not that Tonya was paying any attention to notice, and went to the bedroom to dump his stuff on the bed. "Great to know how much my hard work is appreciated around here," he said to himself as he went back to the kitchen. He had laughed to himself as he had driven home, thinking about how excited Tonya would be to hear of his success. Some good news for a change, he had thought.

♀-♂

Terry and Tonya are the examples for you. Their lives reveal that you have to protect yourself. Terry's response to Tonya's kind gesture was right on. How lame could she be to dare to wash his truck without using the proper soap! Forget about the fact she did something she didn't have to, she did it wrong and that's the point. Her gesture has nothing to do with her, he thought. She didn't think it through or ask him. As well, Tonya's lack of enthusiasm for Terry's announcement was exactly as it should have been. Doesn't Terry realize she has a ton of stuff to do at home and she doesn't have time to listen to whatever he's saying? Could he not see the full dishwasher lying open and the dishes in the sink, and dinner food laid out on the counter? Did he really think she had the time to pay attention to whatever he did at work? Is it her job to stroke his ego and congratulate him for what he should be doing anyway?

Do it like Terry and Tonya. Give no regard for the thought that your spouse does things or says things that reflect how they love, or how they wish to be loved. If you notice how your spouse is always showing appreciation for other's successes, you can ignore this as a clue as to what is meaningful to him. It's not an indication, at all, that perhaps that's how he might wish to receive love. Instead, don't celebrate any of his successes and definitely don't provide any sort of encouragement for what he does or is interested in.

Maybe you notice how your wife constantly wants to talk with you about things that happened during the day. You're tired of how she always mentions "Will you turn off the TV (or put down the magazine, or stop typing on the computer) and look at me, please?" You've heard, "I don't feel you're listening to me," or "I want you to talk with me and hear me," so many times you could puke. That's cool because you are perfectly in the right to be frustrated. She's just trying to suck up your precious time with her rambling. Doesn't she get that you can listen and watch ESPN at the same time?

Why should your full attention be on her while she's talking? What about "me" time for you? And really, most of what she talks about is meaningless descriptions of how her day went, where she went, who she saw, what she did at work, and so on. How can that be more important than you checking your email? Don't give it a second thought. Just continue to partially be engaged and continue doing what you want to do, because that's what really matters—she'll understand.

You probably thought your spouse's habit of collecting toy sports cars was cute when you were dating or even in the first glowing years of your marriage. Now it disgusts you. "How could a grown man get so excited about little metal cars? He's not a little boy anymore," you think. The annual trip to the collector's convention used to be an excuse for vacation away as a couple. But now, you purposely schedule other activities so you don't have to go. Even better, for a week prior to his leaving, deride him and his childish little hobby. Remain in a constant state of frustration that one half of the spare room in your house is consumed by his toy cars. Despite the fact that you've seen him truly happy when he bought a hoped-for car in an online auction, continue to tease him about how stupid it is for him to collect toy cars. Don't let it bother you that your husband is doing something he enjoys. Forget about the fact that he still invites you to go to the convention every year, even though he knows you'll never say yes. If he really wanted to do something together, then why doesn't he take up tennis and play with you, since that's what you like?

You see, for this Surefire Strategy to work, you have to protect yourself. If you're always doing what your spouse enjoys, your own life force will dry up. Your hobbies are a part of who you are; they reflect what is important to you. Shouldn't he notice that, and appreciate it? If your spouse really loved you, she would take interest in what matters to you. So, get prepared to dig in your heels—don't give in and sacrifice what you want just so they can be happy. Protect yourself.

Whatever it is your spouse talks about most, or does the most, or complains that you don't do the most, just ignore. A spouse who is always touching you or letting you know how much she wants to be touched is not, in any way, communicating how she wishes to be loved—it's just neediness. A spouse who gives gifts for just about any occasion is not showing you how he wishes to receive love—he's just trying to buy appreciation. Your spouse wanting to talk all the time is just selfishness—it has nothing to do with how she feels loved. If you're feeling like your spouse should show appreciation for what you do more often, or give you an "attaboy" for your efforts, get over it. You're just fishing for ego-stroking—it has nothing to do with how you feel like she loves you.

♀-♂

Terry and Tonya continued in their ways—not appreciating each other and not being thankful for what the other person did. Without even knowing it, they were working this Strategy to perfection. They actually believed, at the start, that the person they married would see the best in themselves and show appreciation. They bought into the romantic myth that when you make a lifelong vow to someone in marriage, that means each person will be the biggest fan, the loudest cheerleader, and the most supportive friend for the other person. Silly nonsense! As you can see, engaging in that type of behavior means being vulnerable with the person you say you love. It means looking for the best in the other person. To live that romantic myth means a lot of time and it just opens you up for possible hurt and letdown. No, that simply will not do. You must protect yourself at all costs. Do the things you want to do, especially if it comes at the expense of your marriage partner.

By now you're getting the idea, aren't you? If you want to ruin your marriage then don't get involved or show interest in what your spouse is interested in. Better yet, degrade it, antagonize them for it, and ignore it as much as possible. You must protect yourself at all costs. Sacrificing for their betterment or their enjoyment is weak, lame, and is not in your own best interest. Don't do it. Protect yourself. That's the only way this Surefire Strategy will work. And that's exactly what you want, right?

Surefire Strategy #4

That's Your Job!

Live in your strengths. Do only those household tasks that you enjoy doing, if any at all. Forget about "helping out," or "doing your part," or even "pitching in where needed because we're in this together."

You're not a sports team, for crying out loud!

David did what he usually did in these situations: Keep talking and being the gregarious host while his wife Lauren cleared the entire table of dishes. "That's her responsibility. I've got to pay attention to our guests," he thought. Lauren continued making trips back and forth to the kitchen without a word, knowing what David was doing. "He never helps with clearing the table. He just sits there talking, not even saying thank you," she fumed. The more she thought about it, the more she noticed that David refused to help with any of the household chores.

He would come home from his high-powered job as president of a local company and immediately set to the task of reading the mail and catching up on ESPN. Forget about the fact that the kids needed help with their homework, his already-folded laundry needed to be put away, and the dog hadn't been fed. Apparently, anything having to do with the household was her job. David didn't even mess with the yard. A lawn service handled all of the mowing and landscaping. It appeared to Lauren that David believed that since he was bringing home the bacon, it was her responsibility to fry it up in the pan, have enough for kids too, clean up the pan, clear the dishes, and save any bacon for a sandwich later. "Doesn't he know I can't do all this by myself," she thought one morning, while hanging up his towel for the umpteenth time. "Just because I'm not working outside the home doesn't mean I should have to do everything related to the home," she muttered to herself.

David knew what Lauren was thinking as she cleared the dishes. He knew because they had argued about this only last week. "I don't see what the big deal is. I work long hours at the office making sure this family has all the money we need," he remembered thinking after the argument. "Doesn't she get the fact that I don't have the time or energy to do her job for her as well? She's home all day and still expects me to do stuff she should already have finished." Did she really expect that he was going to walk through the door in his $1,000 suit and take the garbage out to the curb? If she had already washed and dried his clothes, was it so hard to put them away? Why did he have to be bothered with that, especially when he had so much work material to think about?

As the guests left for the evening, David thought, "I do my part outside the home. I shouldn't have to come home from working hard and 'do chores.'" As Lauren finished cleaning up the kitchen she thought, "Great! I have to take out the trash too before I can go to bed. I really wish David would help with something around here."

♀-♂

Alicia checked her smartphone for the fourth time in the last ten minutes. "How much longer is this going to take?" she thought. Didn't Steve know she had cases to read over before tomorrow? She quickly read another page of the book for her daughter, kissed her goodnight, and closed little Alice's door. Alicia practically sprinted to her home office before Steve could ask her to help with anything else. She had acquiesced when he had asked her to read to Alice while he washed the dinner dishes. "Why do I let him waste my time like that?" she said with disgust as she closed her office door. "I have work to do—doesn't he see what I bring home every night?"

Steve was fine with being a house-husband. He preferred the term stay-at-home-dad, but he wasn't picky. He had adapted to a new role when he got laid off a year ago, but he was sure that Alicia hadn't even seen that as a blip on her career screen. She was so focused on her work. Granted, she did pull down some serious cash working as a lawyer, but he felt more like her servant or personal assistant than he did her husband. "Ah well, pity party for Steve is over. Time to get to the rest of the evening," he whispered to himself as he swept up the crumbs from under the table.

♀-♂

People will often enter marriage with certain role expectations. My wife will do these tasks, or my husband will do these things.

Typically these expectations are based on what each person saw in their parents. More and more, though, these expectations are based on personal self-interest. As you can see from our two shining examples, you shouldn't have do anything you don't want to do in the household. Role expectations about splitting up the tasks, or the common advice to "share the burden" are the stuff of fairy tales and myths.

If you don't want to take out the garbage then don't be bothered with it. If you're in a marriage where one spouse works outside the home and brings in all of the money for the marriage, then by no means should you have to do any household tasks. You certainly will not be assigned any chores—you're not living in an episode of *The Waltons*. If you both have jobs in the workforce, then be the first to declare what you will not do at home. Stake your ground quickly.

If you're a man, push the stereotypical role expectation of the woman doing the cooking and cleaning. This grants some leverage because if she is doing the cooking, then she should also do the grocery shopping and cleaning up after the cooking. If you're a woman, automatically assume that your husband will take out the garbage, mow the grass, clean the gutters, and do the dishes if you're doing the cooking.

Forget about any advice about "doing your part," "doing your fair share of the work," or "helping out when needed." Always assume that your spouse should be the one doing whatever task needs to be done. After all, you have better stuff to do than some menial chore. Continue to put the expectation on them that they will do it. Under no circumstances should you volunteer to help. Once you do that, you are on the hook for the rest of time. Don't give in.

$♀-♂$

David and Alicia, in their respective marriages, have this Surefire Strategy down pat. Not only are actions in perfect form, their mindset is right on target. You have to think it before you can enact it. By taking the superiority angle, David could keep Lauren at bay. If she started pushing back too much, then he could just work more and be gone more. Alicia worked the superiority angle as well, with some added "What-I-do-is-more-valuable-than-what-you-do" irritation to keep picking at Steve.

Meanwhile, their spouses were stuck holding on to the nonsense notion that the people they married would actually help them in what they were doing in their lives. Lauren continued to believe that David would notice how much work she had running the household and offer to pitch in and help out of love. Silly Lauren! Steve never quite grasped that asking Alicia to help with anything in the home was equal to asking her to quit her job. Silly Steve! Lauren and Steve, in their respective marriages, were still holding to the notion of "We're in this together, so let's pull together and make it through together!" Don't they understand their marriages are not a sports team?

If David didn't feel like doing anything when he got home from a hard day's work, then he shouldn't have to. If Alicia believed that her work as a lawyer trumped anything Steve might ask of her, then that's the way it had to be. David and Alicia are shining examples of seeing marriage not as a partnership where both partners share responsibilities, but rather as hierarchy, where one person does a lot of work to make a lot of money and the other person in the marriage does the rest.

You need to begin thinking like David, or Alicia. Helping out with household tasks is for the weak. You be strong. Always think of what you do as the most important, and continually look at what your spouse does as secondary, if not unimportant in comparison. Having this mindset firmly entrenched will aid your living out this Surefire Strategy. In regards to chores always take the position that it's your spouse's job to handle the chore, not yours. Never volunteer to help your spouse with something. Don't ever utter the words, "Is there anything I can help you with today?" Automatically assume that you will do whatever you wish to do when you are home. Push back against any attempts to get you to do tasks you don't want to do. Turn those attempts into knock-down arguments if needed, but you must get the message to your spouse that "helping out" isn't going to be happening.

If you can successfully enact this Surefire Strategy, you, like David and Alicia, will be well on your way to ruining your relationship with your spouse.

Surefire Strategy #5

They're Only Pictures!

Definitely get into porn.

Skip subscribing to a magazine. Get it instantly online.

Make sure you view it daily. Use it instead of a real, intimate, sexual experience with your spouse because that's always the same thing, same position (and not very often!). Better yet, just take the natural next step and have an affair.

It's just sex, after all.

She got into the minivan expecting to have an enjoyable ride to the mountains with her women's tennis doubles team. The four of them were getting away for the weekend to relax and spend time together. They weren't too far down the road before the driver said, "I've got some entertainment for us for the drive up," as she hit the DVD button on the console. Within minutes a porn movie was playing on the same screen her children usually watched Dora the Explorer. The other moms in the van were enthralled with the moans and copulations on the screen. Diane, however, was stunned. She never imagined that these soccer-mom-minivan-driving-tennis-playing women would be interested in pornography. She cringed when she heard one of the women in the van say, "Maybe I should show this to my husband on our next trip!"

♀-♂

Susan flipped through one of the many women's magazines she received as she waited for her children to come home from school. She believed she had a good marriage but "30 Ways to Spark Your Marriage" got her attention as she turned a page. Skimming through the tips, she paused when she read the one about "steamy visuals." The tip was to get a porn movie and show it to your husband and then have rip-roaring sex. "The visual action will definitely get him turned on—and who knows, maybe you'll pick up some moves of your own to try," she read. She'd never had any trouble getting Jim turned on before this so she wasn't sure she needed any "help."

♀-♂

Don liked to work in his home office. Carla appreciated the fact that he was home a lot and could get the kids off the bus in the afternoon. She felt good about their marriage, even if they hadn't had as much sex lately. As she chopped celery for the dinner salad, she reasoned with herself—it wasn't like she was wanting to get laid every day, but she did enjoy the physical action and release and closeness she felt with Don, she just wanted it more than once a month. As easily as she brushed her hair out of her eyes, she brushed the thought away and called to Don in his office that dinner was about ready.

Don liked to work in his home office. It was in a back corner of the house and gave him immense privacy for his calls and allowed him to concentrate on his work. It also gave him free reign to surf for porn for hours a day. He had installed special features on his browser to hide his internet history and erase it quickly, but he thought that was overkill, as Carla never came to his office and had her own computer in the front of the house. He never really thought about why he started looking for porn. He had been attracted to Carla and still found her good-looking—her long tan legs and doe eyes continued to draw admiring stares. He liked that he had an attractive wife. But one day he happened upon a pop-up and curiosity got the best of him and off he went. These women he saw were gorgeous and were in so many positions—none of which Carla had ever tried. He clicked and clicked into world after world of fantasy sex. He was so turned on he had sex with himself right there in his computer chair. He tried to turn that lust to his wife that evening, but she couldn't seem to keep up with the images in his mind. Don kept doing "business" in his office, all the while Carla thinking proudly of him for how focused he was on his work.

It wasn't too long before Carla's long tan legs and doe eyes weren't really doing anything for Don. He stopped touching her and sex was the furthest thing from his mind, unless it was with himself and all his internet porn women. All he had to do was click and another would be there on his screen. Carla noticed his lack of intimacy and physical interaction with her, but wrote it off for a couple of months to Don working hard. She still felt a bit neglected but figured it was a very short-term thing and didn't make much of it.

Three months down the line, however, she began to mention to Don that she missed having sex with him. He responded that he had a lot of work to do and was just too tired all the time. She heard him but in her mind she had a twitch of doubt. She began to notice that he spent hours and hours in his home office. Before,

Don would come out every couple of hours to stretch his legs or grab some lunch or just chat with her. Now, he went to his office before nine in the morning and emerged quickly at lunchtime to get a sandwich and hurry back to his office to eat. He wouldn't emerge until dinner time. Carla began to wonder about these changes.

One day, Don had a dentist appointment and Carla decided to explore his office. She felt a little guilty that she was spying on her husband, but he had been acting differently, which is to say negatively. Don apparently had become quite bold in his thinking that Carla would never enter his office because he left his computer on when he departed to his appointment. As Carla moved the mouse to erase the screen saver, the screen filled with the images Don had just been viewing. Stunned, she didn't touch anything else and ran from his office to their bedroom upstairs and cried on the bed.

More and more people are viewing porn for leisure purposes these days. Some studies have shown up to 70 percent of men view porn monthly, with 50 percent viewing it weekly. Interestingly, more and more women are buying porn and using it, upwards of 30 percent.[1] The stigma it once had seems to be fading. Now, porn is seen as just another sex tool—use it to spice up your marriage, or get you both turned on for each other, or for research you can use in bed in the future. So, what are you waiting for? Jump on the bandwagon and get your porn fix today!

Don't worry about the fuddy-duddies who say it's harmful to your relationship because it's fake and manufactured and creates unrealistic expectations. It's just the prudes who talk about how viewing pornography separates the physical and emotional components of sex from actual sex. They go on and on about how viewing porn makes people less sensitive toward women, turns them into objects, and increases aggressive behavior. You want what you

---

[1] See www.thecrimson.com/article/2011/3/28/porn-pornography-moral-doeful/, accessed March 28, 2011.

want. Spicing up your marriage by bringing in a third-party (even if it's a video) is precisely the way to strengthen the intimate bond with your spouse. Don't worry about the naysayers who declare that people who look at porn have a harder time experiencing healthy relationships, or that they tend to experience less sexual satisfaction over time. You're looking at attractive men and women engaging in a variety of sex—there's no way you'll get bored with your spouse's body or need more and more porn to continue to feel "spicy." Uptight people will pontificate that porn users are increasingly unable to connect emotional involvement with sex, but don't let that stop you from surfing to picture after picture of booty, boobs, and blow jobs.

Of course, you have the save-all argument ready to go when anyone may mention that viewing porn is somehow morally wrong. "It doesn't hurt anyone because it's just private viewing pleasure," you can retort. There will be others who will agree with you, as half of young women don't see anything morally wrong with viewing porn and upwards of two-thirds of men see no problem with it.[2] Sure, those folks haven't made a lifetime commitment in marriage, but don't worry about that. Just because porn affects the deepest part of your brain when you view it, don't let that reality get in your way of getting turned on by an anonymous person on your computer screen.

Using someone else to turn you on so that then, and only then, you will be able to have sex with your spouse, doesn't interfere with the vow to be true and honor only your spouse at all. It's just a picture, right? That really doesn't do any damage to the trust and intimacy of your relationship with your spouse. It doesn't hurt him or her. Because, of course, your spouse knows you're just viewing porn so you can have steamier sex with him or her, right? You've told them that's what you're doing so it's not a secret, is it? If it doesn't really hurt anyone, then you don't need to surf the internet in secret anymore, just do it with your spouse right next to you—it'll be a great foreplay exercise.

[2]   Ibid.

You want to spice up your marriage so it makes perfect sense to use the totally staged sexual antics of complete strangers to achieve that goal. You could just ask your neighbors to come and have sex in your living room while you watch and that would do the same thing, but hey, you don't want to impose, so just dial up a porn video—it won't do any damage to your relationship. Don't use your own imagination and actually talk with your spouse about trying some new positions or communicate what really matters to you in sex, just watch other people having sex and that will be just the ticket to sexual success with your spouse.

For sure, don't let yourself enjoy the natural progression of sex through the different stages of life with your spouse. Embrace boredom and lazy relational skills and experience sexual release with an image or a printed page instead of with the man or woman you pledged to be faithful to. Ignore the familiarity you have of knowing your spouse's smell and favorite body spots, of knowing that this person you're having sex with accepts the best and worst of you and still wants to have sex with you. Simply invite Nikki and Dirk from the porn video into your marriage because that's what you both had in mind when you stood together, said your vows, and got married. Don't worry about pornography leading you to stray away from your spouse, either emotionally or physically. Viewing other people having sex is always good for cementing your commitment to the man or woman you're <u>not</u> watching on the video.

♀-♂

Look at what viewing porn did for Don and Carla's marriage: Carla's confidence was crushed and her trust of her husband was demolished. Don grew more and more distant from his wife to the point that he left her for another woman (and that relationship didn't last very long either). See, viewing pornography is exactly what your marriage needs. After all, it doesn't really do any harm to the marriage or to your spouse, right?

Surefire Strategy #6

I Married You, Not Them!

Ignore your spouse's family—they're not who you married.

Don't call, text, or email on special occasions like birthdays or anniversaries.

For your own sake, make every effort to avoid family gatherings at holiday times, especially reunions. Remember to neglect any issues regarding your spouse's siblings or aging parents.

Kaitlyn married Sean. Kaitlyn did not, in her mind, marry Sean's family, whom she didn't like. His parents were still alive which meant Kaitlyn would have to face interactions with them from time to time. She knew this prior to marrying him, but she had made up her mind that she was not going to enjoy these interactions.

Kaitlyn thanked her lucky stars when Sean got transferred 700 miles away from his family. She knew this would greatly decrease her socializing with them. Who knows? Perhaps she would be so lucky that she'd only have to see them once a year at most. Meanwhile, she would slip derogatory comments about Sean's parents into conversation. Sean put up with it because he didn't want to live that close to his parents either, but it still ate at him because they were his parents, after all.

It wasn't like he was a momma's boy or anything, but Sean did like to see his family more than once a year. Maybe it was just nostalgia, but he enjoyed hearing the stories and the feel of being with his siblings. Kaitlyn's cutting remarks didn't bother him much at first, but over several months, her putdowns were wearing him down. Did she really have to make fun of how his family celebrated Christmas every year? Was it necessary for her to joke about the meal that was served out of tradition each Christmas Eve? Sean found he was growing more and more irritated with Kaitlyn.

Kaitlyn did her best to keep up the criticism. When Sean actually floated the idea of having his mom and dad come to visit in the summer, she threw a fit. There was no way in hell she was going to have his parents in her house. She didn't even want them in her city. While Sean quickly backed down, Kaitlyn kept up her defenses on this issue for the next several weeks, repeatedly telling Sean how foolish he was for suggesting such a stupid idea.

♀-♂

You should be able to see where Kaitlyn and Sean are headed, relationship-wise. Their destination is yours as well if you choose to use this Surefire Strategy. Kaitlyn is spot on for sticking to her guns about Sean's family coming to visit. She also is doing a fabulous job of letting her husband know how much she doesn't like his family. Her efforts will not go unrewarded, to be sure.

Take a page from Kaitlyn's playbook and get to work. Make your spouse's family out to be the enemy. Find anyway at all to be critical of them, and don't be shy about keeping your opinion to yourself—let your spouse hear about it often. Don't ever have your spouse's siblings or parents stay in your house, or come to visit, even if it means having to pay for a hotel. You don't want them nosing around your home and making suggestions about anything. Keep them at arm's length as much as possible. That way it will always be a chore to actually go to where they are living. Hopefully, you are not living in close proximity to your in-laws. If you are, try to find some reason, any reason, to move as far away as possible.

Perhaps moving away is not an option, and you are stuck living close to them. You'll have to adapt to the current conditions then. For instance, if you have no choice but to make an appearance, keep it brief and antagonistic. Make sure your spouse's family doesn't like you much, but will "put up with you for the sake of their son or daughter." Keep communication to a minimum, especially with your spouse's parents. The more they try to talk to you, the more you should resist. If you let them get to know you, or start to form meaningful relationship with you, chances increase that you'll slip and be vulnerable with them. When that happens, they get a hold into your life and your emotions. You must avoid this situation from happening at all costs, or this Strategy will not work at all. Resist. Reject. Repeat.

Keeping your in-laws at arm's length is more accessible than you think. Activities or behaviors you might engage in for people you actually care anything about, you simply do not do with your in-laws. Never buy a birthday gift or anniversary gift for your in-laws. If there's no way to get out of being at the party or celebration, then stay off by yourself or watch a game in another room while the party is going on. If it's your spouse's parent's birthday, be sure to make cracks like, "Too many more birthdays and we'll be getting the inheritance early!" It almost goes without saying that you will not be purchasing Christmas gifts or stocking stuffers for your spouse's family, but I don't want you to forget that easy step. Keep your cellphone number secret or always ignore their calls—they'll get the idea soon enough. Don't text, email, tweet, or allow any of your spouse's family on your Facebook page. You do not want them "friending" you! While the above paragraph provides you with a few no-brainer ideas to get this Strategy in place, some other situations may take a bit more finesse on your part.

If your spouse's family gathers at holidays, be the strong silent type at the dinner table, or basically aloof at most other times. Keep the conversation at surface issues. Don't share your feelings about, really, anything of substance. Pay attention to family culture so you can use it to your advantage. For example, if politics and religion are not talked about a lot, be sure to bring up the topics at random times, just to force the issue. And don't forget to take the opposite side of your spouse's family. If they are die-hard Democrats, then be a raving, right-wing Republican in your conversations. This Surefire Strategy will take more effort on your part, but the payoff is worth it. You cannot truly ruin your relationship with the one you married if you do not attack his or her family.

As you can see, your goal is generally to make an ass of yourself with your spouse's family. They need to understand that you married their child, not them. Their son or daughter is your husband or wife and that's really the only connection. Your life with your spouse is *your* life, not theirs. They don't need to know "how things are going," or whether you're expecting a child yet, or if finances are tight or not. The two of you can make it on your own, without their help, without their advice or money, and certainly without their meddling into your relationship. "Leaving and cleaving" is not just some biblical cliché.

One final area is worthy of mention here, but it does not apply across the board for every relationship. However, if your spouse has aging parents, then the possibilities are ripe for ways to use that to your advantage.

Absolutely don't let your spouse's mother or father stay with you. Refuse any attempts to build or convert a room to an "in-law" suite. Just like with having your spouse's parents come to visit, you must remain diligent against having actually live under the same roof as you. If you allow this because of misguided compassion or silly weakness, they will steal all attention away from you. If your spouse is a momma's boy or a daddy's girl, know from the start that their relationship will hone in on yours from time to time, especially at the end of life. Nay, nay, stay away. You have to be firm in this area. You have to keep your in-laws out of your life, even if they are at the end of their life. If your spouse has siblings, point out that they should be shouldering the burden of care for their parents instead. Do. Not. Give. In.

Can you be like Kaitlyn? She is your role model on this Strategy. As long as you can be unrelenting and stay on focus, you shouldn't experience any failure by using this Strategy. But, if you give in or falter even a little, you will make it harder for yourself, so keep your eye on the prize. Don't let distractions like your spouse crying, or your in-laws getting angry with you pull you off focus. You cannot let their feelings intrude on what you're doing. You will have to ignore their emotions and continue with the criticism and ignoring behavior. Resist. Reject. Repeat. Do this and you will successfully employ this Strategy in ruining your relationship with your spouse. Which is exactly what you're after, right?

Surefire Strategy #7

Are They Coming Over Again?

Since when do you have to be chummy with their friends?

Make excuses for why you can't make it to Zach and Jennifer's party.

When they want to have their group of friends over, be nasty about it, or schedule something else on top of it.

Ryan had Susan fooled. She believed he was really interested in her, and by extension, in her friends. When they got married she just knew that they would have good times with her friends, socializing, eating, and partying. Ryan played along, stringing her along. He had no attention of hanging out with her friends because he didn't really like them. It wasn't until after they were married that he started the attacks. Cutting remarks about how her friends looked increased weekly. He kept refusing to go to dinner engagements. He only wanted to use her for sex and he believed that her friends were getting in the way of that desire.

Whether it was blind love or just dumb naiveté, Susan kept trying to believe the best about her husband, but it was really hard. She attempted to meet with her friends alone but she felt odd not having Ryan with her, especially since they were newlyweds. Being the only "uncoupled" woman in a crowd of married couples was just too awkward for her. Susan wanted to enjoy going out with her husband, not pulling a quasi-single routine again—she was married!

It didn't even take one year and Ryan had worn Susan down. She stopped asking friends over for coffee and dessert, and repeatedly turned down offers from other couples to come over for dinner or parties. In less than a year, Ryan had achieved great success with this Surefire Strategy—he and Susan divorced less than 11 months after their wedding date. He didn't just ruin the relationship, he crushed it! Ryan's success is your goal. Just because your spouse enjoys doing stuff with other people doesn't mean you have to. Be like Ryan.

♀-♂

When your husband schedules a night out with the guys, give him grief about it all day long, and especially the morning after. Say things like, "Great, you're choosing to go out with your boys instead of being at home with your wonderful wife—thanks for making me feel like I'm secondhand." If your wife plans a lunch with her girlfriends, bitch and moan about being all alone at home. Further, complain about what stuff needs to be done while she's out. Make snide remarks like, "I'm so glad you want to ignore me. You never want to have lunch with me." Part of the secret of this Strategy is acting like a bratty, whiny child, but there is such power there. Don't let a little immaturity stand in your way of unleashing the full force of this Surefire Strategy. Besides, your behavior will only be temporary until you achieve your goal. Whatever your situation may be, your goal is to make your spouse feel guilty about enjoying an activity with someone other than you.

You don't want your spouse to forge relationships with their friends because that will mean sharing stories about marriage and that leads to comparisons. You don't want to spend much time with other couples because that also leads to the inevitable comparisons. Comparisons are bad, except when you can compare your spouse to some botoxed, airbrushed famous person that your spouse won't ever stand a chance of measuring up to. Then, however, comparisons are okay. But generally, you don't want your spouse comparing you to other spouses, or to have your marriage be juxtaposed with another marriage. As much as possible, you want all of your spouse's attention on you, not being diluted by interactions with their friends.

♀-♂

This was Krista's third marriage, so she'd had good success in ending marriages. Her marriage to Jackson started well enough, all lovey-dovey romance. But it wasn't too long before her well-honed knack for being critical kicked in with his other relationships. Jackson had some close friends that he enjoyed socializing with from time to time. Jackson's friends were married and single, male and female—a nice, well-rounded bunch. Krista put up with these gatherings for as long as she could stand it, but eventually, she started to point out how Jackson's buddy Tom had put on some weight. She especially got catty when she constantly remarked about how Jackson's friend Martika had saggy boobs.

Jackson attempted to deflect these comments but he found he couldn't do it. He began to create ways to meet his friends without

Krista, but she still was critical. It got so bad that he no longer looked forward to meeting his friends because of the crap he knew he'd receive when he got home. So, he began begging off invitations and turning down parties. Krista was winning! He just couldn't understand why she had to act so nasty toward his friends.

Krista found she felt better about herself when she pointed out the faults and imperfections of other people. It seemed that's how she handled any stress in her life—criticize others, especially if she had any type of relationship with them. Besides, she felt that since Jackson had married her, he should want to spend most, if not all of his time with her. His old friendships should pass to the wayside. When he professed his undying love for her in the wedding ceremony, Krista believed that meant investing time with her that he had previously invested in his various friendships. Didn't he understand that it was about the two of them together? Why couldn't he grasp the fact that his friendships were just keeping him from living out his love for her? Krista had to keep up the attacks in order to shake his mind loose and see the new reality.

Their relationship continued for a while longer in quiet misery, but after a couple of years, it seemed that Krista could add a third marriage to her destruction belt. Jackson didn't so much give up as give out. He had no more energy to withstand the life-sucking force of Krista's constant barrage.

♀-♂

You don't need to be only a man, or only a woman to use this Surefire Strategy—its success is not gender-based. As Ryan and Krista, respectively, show, you can rag on your spouse's friends regardless. Ryan was perhaps more devious, but his obstinate stance works. Just keep saying no to any requests for parties and dinners. Make it so awkward for your spouse to meet his or her friends alone that he or she will begin to turn down those invitations. Then you have your spouse doing your job for you! Once that happens, you'll know the tide has turned and you should be able to surf on out of the relationship.

Krista's approach also will be successful. Criticism of your spouse's friends works as good as being stubborn about social invites. In order to be really good with Krista's approach, you will need to harken your memory back to middle school and high school. A stroll down memory lane will help you recall how to be catty about appearance, how to be vindictive over the smallest social slight, and how to be critical and nit-picky. If your spouse, or one of their friends tells you you're being immature, celebrate because it means you are in the sweet zone of sarcasm. If you hear a retort, "Quit acting like a 12-year-old," then absorb it with a smile. You'll only be emboldened to ramp up the comments and unasked-for critiques. Just because others accuse you of pouting, whining, or even acting like a jerk, doesn't mean you should stop employing this Strategy. If anything, you should increase what you're doing because the comments tell you you've hit the right button.

You've got to stick to the belief that friends don't help a marriage, they water it down with their pandering influence. Who needs friends when you and your spouse have each other? Don't their friends understand the traditional phrase, "leaving and cleaving?" How can your spouse's friends not comprehend the truth that if you had wanted to spend a lot of time with them you would have moved all together to a compound in the country and lived communally? If you had really wanted to spend that much time together you would have all moved to the same apartment complex or bought homes in the same neighborhood. Can they not take a hint? This is one of the hardest Strategies because, typically, your spouse will have many friends, who each represent a threat to your spouse's attention toward you. Keep those threats to a minimum, if not totally eliminated.

You may have doubts about whether you can employ this Strategy fully. After all, who looks forward to returning, emotionally, to when they were 14? But you must. You'll get criticized when you're in the meaty part of this Strategy, but refuse to let it get in your way. Once you start, it really does get easier to complain about your spouse's friends, whine about how much time your spouse spends with them, and zing biting criticism toward anyone your spouse knew before marrying you. Keep focused! Build walls between you and your spouse's friends. Make sure to put distance between them and your spouse, then increase that distance any way possible. You've got to get your spouse's attention off of their previous friendships and on to you. If you can successfully slice their friends off the social radar, then you are well on your way to ruining your relationship—just like you've wanted!

Final Word

Will This Really Work?

*You must be dedicated to killing your marriage
for these Surefire Strategies to work properly.*

If you've read this far, you now have the secret knowledge of how to effectively ruin your relationship with your spouse. If you are merely engaged, you can use these strategies as well, with a bit more effort, and save yourself the hassle of getting married in the first place. Plus you'll save all that money on the ceremony, reception, rehearsal dinner, and of course, the honeymoon. Quite a savings there!

You can only be a Marriage Killer when you put the Surefire Strategies to work. Just reading about them won't do you any good, other than give you marriage-killing thoughts. Also, when you enact these Strategies, you have to give 100% toward the effort. Don't go about this halfway, or mildly, or tentatively. Your goal is to kill your marriage. That requires you to use your chosen Strategy will full force. Go back and read about the actual people who used these Strategies successfully. Do they look like people who were distracted from their goal? Do they come across as men or women who were only "sort-of" employing these Strategies? No!

If you go about this with a half-assed attitude, you'll only succeed in creating more tension, negativity, or stress, but you won't successfully kill your marriage. You'll just make it more miserable.

The Seven Surefire Strategies are to help you. They are tools you can successfully use to ruin your relationship. This is not about breaking up, separating, "taking a break," "giving each other some space," growing apart, "taking a vacation from the relationship," working through it, or "giving time to get your mind refocused." This is about killing your marriage! You're not attempting to just make it more antagonistic or tension-filled. You are setting out to kill your marriage! Destroy it! Ruin it! Bust it wide open! Kill it!

Thoughts of love for your spouse need to find some other place to roost. Caring about how this will shake out with your spouse needs to be eliminated from your heart. Wondering if they will be okay has no place in your mind if you're going to use Marriage Killers the way it is intended to be used. You're not trying to build up or strengthen your relationship—you are seeking to ruin it completely so you can get on with *your* life, *your* dreams, *your* needs, and *your* wants. Remember, this is all about you!

After all, that's really what you want, isn't it?

Acknowledgements

For all of the couples described in this book, I thank you. Literally, without your escapades and lame behavior, this book would not have been possible.

For the early readers who gave feedback and critique prior to publication: thank you for sharing your thoughts. This book is better because of you.

To those readers who have contacted me with comments about the focus, purpose, and tone of Marriage Killers, I appreciate knowing where your heart is and how you think. Feel free to follow other news about Marriage Killers at www.marriagekillers.org

Finally, for my wife: My love, I am so thankful that neither of us seek to employ these Strategies in our marriage. Thank you for being the woman I love with all I am, and thank you for loving me with all of who you are. Always and forever!

About the Author

Combine *Daily Show*-type sarcasm with the alarming frequency of couples splitting and you get Dr. John Page's *Marriage Killers*. Drawing from more than 15 years of experience and training, Dr. Page has witnessed the stupid choices people make in their marital relationships and wants you to learn from them. He has lectured from coast-to-coast in the US, as well as Australia, Argentina, Cuba, Peru, and the United Kingdom. His work has appeared in regional publications in Atlanta, Lexington, and Tulsa. He and his wife and children live in Georgia.

Visit

www.marriagekillers.org